SandCastle™
Mini Animal Marvels

Miniature Mammals

A Division of ABDO
ABDO
Publishing Company

Alex Kuskowski   Consulting Editor, Diane Craig, M.A./Reading Specialist

visit us at www.abdopublishing.com

Published by ABDO Publishing Company, a division of ABDO, P.O. Box 398166, Minneapolis, Minnesota 55439. Copyright © 2014 by Abdo Consulting Group, Inc. International copyrights reserved in all countries. No part of this book may be reproduced in any form without written permission from the publisher. SandCastle™ is a trademark and logo of ABDO Publishing Company.

Printed in the United States of America, North Mankato, Minnesota
102013
012014

 PRINTED ON RECYCLED PAPER

Editor: Liz Salzmann
Content Developer: Alex Kuskowski
Cover and Interior Design and Production: Mighty Media, Inc.
Photo Credits: Shutterstock, Mike Richardson

Library of Congress Cataloging-in-Publication Data

Kuskowski, Alex.
  Miniature mammals / Alex Kuskowski.
     pages cm. -- (Mini animal marvels)
  ISBN 978-1-62403-067-3
1. Mammals--Juvenile literature. 2. Mammals--Size--Juvenile literature. I. Title.
  QL706.2.K87 2014
  599--dc23
                    2013022903

SandCastle™ Level: Transitional

SandCastle™ books are created by a team of professional educators, reading specialists, and content developers around five essential components—phonemic awareness, phonics, vocabulary, text comprehension, and fluency—to assist young readers as they develop reading skills and strategies and increase their general knowledge. All books are written, reviewed, and leveled for guided reading, early reading intervention, and Accelerated Reader® programs for use in shared, guided, and independent reading and writing activities to support a balanced approach to literacy instruction. The SandCastle™ series has four levels that correspond to early literacy development. The levels are provided to help teachers and parents select appropriate books for young readers.

Emerging Readers
(no flags)

Beginning Readers
(1 flag)

Transitional Readers
(2 flags)

Fluent Readers
(3 flags)

Table of Contents

Miniature Mammals

Miniature **mammals** are small animals. They include foxes, hedgehogs, mice, and deer.

Fennec Fox

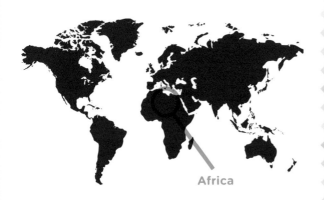

Africa

The fennec fox is the smallest fox. It lives in the desert. It has very big ears.

It is 16 inches
(40.6 cm) long.

6 feet
(1.8 m)

16 inches
(40.6 cm)

The fennec fox hears animals **underground**. It digs to catch them.

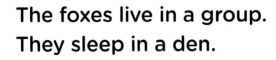

The foxes live in a group.
They sleep in a den.

African Pygmy Hedgehog

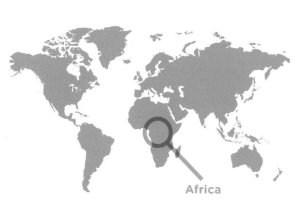

Africa

African pygmy
hedgehogs can be pets.
People all over the
world have hedgehogs.

6 feet
(1.8 m)

It is 8 inches
(20.3 cm) long.

8 inches
(20.3 cm)

Pygmy hedgehogs are very active. They move around a lot. They eat bugs.

African Pygmy Mouse

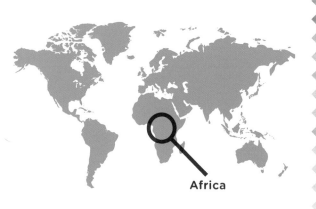

Africa

The African pygmy mouse is the smallest mouse. Some people keep them as pets.

6 feet
(1.8 m)

It is 3 inches
(7.6 cm) long.

3 inches
(7.6 cm)

African pygmy mice lick dew. That is how they drink. They eat bugs and seeds.

Pudú

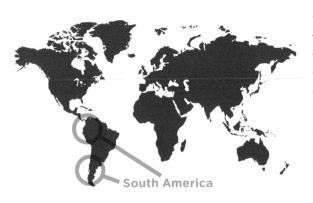

South America

The Pudú is the smallest deer. It lives in the **rain forest**. It lives alone.

6 feet
(1.8 m)

It is 17 inches
(43.2 cm) tall.

17 inches
(43.2 cm)

Pudús eat plants.
They eat grass and leaves.

Did You Know?

 Fennec foxes sleep during the day.

 A hedgehog will curl into a ball when it's scared.

 African pygmy mice live for two years.

 **Male** pudús have antlers.

Mammal Quiz

1 The fennec fox hears animals moving **underground**.

2 Pygmy hedgehogs are not very active.

3 The African pygmy mouse licks dew to drink water.

4 Pudús live in the desert.

5 Pudús eat grass and leaves.

Glossary

antler – a bony growth on the head of an animal in the deer family.

male – being of the sex that can father offspring. Fathers are male.

mammal – a warm-blooded animal that has hair and whose females produce milk to feed their young.

rain forest – a tropical wooded area that gets a lot of rain and has very tall trees.

underground – below the surface of the earth.